[Iconographia]

a Franco Maria Ricci edition

UMBERTO BRUNELLESCHI

*fashion-stylist, illustrator,
stage and costume designer*

Introduction by
Cristina Nuzzi

RIZZOLI
NEW YORK

The Publisher and Cristina Nuzzi would like to thank Sir Harold Acton, Franca Ghelingani, widow of Umberto Brunelleschi, Celio Brunelleschi, Folco Lazzaroni Brunelleschi, Giuseppe Chigiotti and the Directors of the Teatro Comunale of Florence for permission to photograph and publish works reproduced in this volume.

Designed by Franco Maria Ricci
Edited by Laura Casalis
Translated from the Italian by Katherine Benita Wells
Photographs by Valerio Signorini, Florence
Colour separations by Litoffset, Milan
Text composed in Bodoni Italics
Printed in Milan by Grafiche Milani, June 1979.
Published in the United States of America by
RIZZOLI INTERNATIONAL PUBLICATIONS, INC.
712 Fifth Avenue/New York 10019

Library of Congress Catalog Card Number: 79-88271
ISBN: 0-8478-0255-8
Printed in Italy.

Introduction

The renewed interest in recent years in Art Nouveau and Art Deco graphics has led to a partial rediscovery of the work of Umberto Brunelleschi[1], Tuscan by birth but Parisian by adoption, who worked in Paris from 1900 until his death in 1949. Yet his activities as a painter and above all as a costume and set designer, in our opinion the most important of all, which were carried out mainly in Paris but also in Germany, America, and Italy, are still practically unknown. It is this work that makes him, after Léon Bakst (1866-1924) and alongside the Russians Alexander Benois (1870-1960) and Erté (1892–) and the Frenchmen Georges Barbier (1882-1932) and Georges Lepape (1887-1971) – the last two are also due for rediscovery – a leading figure in the history of theatrical costume and twentieth-century scenography.

Born at Montemurlo, near Pistoia, on 21 June, 1879, the son of Arascilde Brunelleschi, an insurance agent, and his wife Benedetta Cappelli, Umberto studied at the Accademia di Belle Arti in Florence under Ciaranfi and Sorbi[2]; but the unchanging and stalely academic climate in Florence at the end of the last century failed to satisfy him, while the myth of artistic life and society in the Ville Lumière, which in 1900 was reaching the height of its prestige with the excitement caused by the Exposition Universelle, exercised a great attraction for him.

So Umberto Brunelleschi decided to move to Paris, Mecca of artists of every nationality since the middle of the nineteenth century.

News of the intellectual flowering and exuberance

Femme au Perroquet (*Woman with a Parrot*), *tempera on canvas, 1903/1905, Rome, private collection.*

7

of ideas and movements in the French capital had
been reaching Tuscany since the time of the Macchiaioli,
but without causing much stir. Telemaco Signorini,
who was in Paris after 1870, knew the works of
Degas and Manet and had even been somewhat
influenced by them; Diego Martelli, friend and
supporter of the Macchiaioli, had tried, without
success, to spread the principles of Impressionism
through his critical writings[3], and had even sent two
of Pissarro's paintings to the Florentine Exhibition in
1878; later on, between 1890 and 1895, the young
Leghorn painter Alfredo Muller (1869-1940)[4],
who was frequently in Paris after 1878, provided
constant information on the latest events in artistic
Paris, but his words went almost unheeded.
When Umberto Brunelleschi reached Paris in 1900,
together with Ardengo Soffici, Giovanni Costetti
and Gino Melis[5], the art of the Impressionists had
long been in decline and Symbolist and
neo-Impressionist trends, though at their peak, were being
overtaken by new tendencies. Within a short time the
"Fauve" movement and then Picasso's and Braque's
Cubism were to steer art in other directions.
For a young newcomer to Paris who was rich in
talent but poor in financial resources, one of the
easiest and quickest ways of earning a living was to
work for an illustrated paper. Wall decoration,
books (this was a time of numbered luxury editions),
and illustrated papers were burgeoning everywhere.
Outstanding among the magazines were Le Rire,
Gil Blas, Frou-Frou, L'Assiette au Beurre, and
Charivari. These publications received drawings from
the chief French illustrators of the day, many of
whom were inspired by Toulouse-Lautrec, like
Abel Faivre, Charles Léandre, Hermann-Paul, Sem,
Willette, Louis Morin, Louis Forain, Henri Somm,
as well as from foreigners such as the Portuguese
Léal da Camara, the Russian Caran d'Ache,
the Swiss Steinlen and the Tuscan Leonetto
Cappiello, who had come to Paris in 1898 and

Self-protrait with a Hat, *60x60 cm., oils on canvas, 1904,
Pegli, private collection.*

quickly made a name for himself as a cartoonist and "maître de l'affiche". These illustrations were mainly humourous – political and social satire – and were sometimes mildly pornographic.

In June 1902 Brunelleschi started working for L'Assiette au Beurre, which had started the previous year and had been received enthusiastically by the public. He made his debut in a special issue called "La Foire au Croûtes" which satirized the fashionable painters of the moment. Brunelleschi did the caricatures, while the other contributor to the paper, the young Paul Iribe[6], was the author of mock tableaux.

These caricatures showed how Brunelleschi had matured through his contact with Parisian influences: his combinations of light and shadow, almost like those of a photographic negative, were similar to Caran d'Ache; his line was close to the manner of Jossot; and his distortion of lineaments and features showed an affinity with the Portuguese Léal da Camara, another frequent contributor to L'Assiette au Beurre (but Brunelleschi's style was clean, while that of the Portuguese illustrator was blurred). These early works were signed with a pseudonym, Harun-al-Rashid, borrowed from the Thousand and One Nights. It was not long before L'Assiette au Beurre, the staff of which now included about forty important names including Abel Faivre, Léandre Steinlen, Caran d'Ache, and Cappiello already mentioned, and Georges Meunier, Vallotton, Villon, and van Dongen, asked Brunelleschi to do the illustrations for the 27 September issue entitled "Nos Musiciens". In some of these illustrations the young Tuscan showed that he had already reached a high degree of independence and finesse.

The depiction of Giacomo Puccini, showing the composer curiously hidden between his collar and his hat, is an example: broad colour washes (grey, white, black, and pink) cut by extraordinarily fine and elegant lines.

Robe de promenade en Surah à damiers et taffetas peint à la main, bordée de velours noir. Chapeau de paille orné d'un panache en duvet de Cygne.

Fashion sketch for the "Journal des Dames et des Modes", engraving coloured "au pochoir", 1912.

But graphic work was not Brunelleschi's only occupation. He had also decided to go on with his painting: the evocative Self Portrait with a Hat, done in 1904, which, in its subdued colouring, its dense pictorial texture, and three-quarters view, was influenced by North European cultures enjoying great favour in Paris, proved to be a good start. Brunelleschi had already taken part in the 1903 Paris salons, and in 1906 he sent to the Salon des Indépendants a portrait of his mother. Guillaume Apollinaire called it "sérieusement executé"[7] and others rightly discerned (in its two-dimensional composition and marked decorative quality) the influence of the American Whistler. The same influence may be seen in the beautiful portrait of Signora Rosenval (1906), now lost; it recalled the suppleness of Japanese painting, filtered through the interpretations of the Symbolists and Nabis, and showed a distinct predilection for languid atmosphere, touched with decadent melancholy. Whistler had considerably influenced[8] many artists in Paris, particularly during his last stay there, when he had even opened (in 1898) an art school, l'Académie Carmen.

Scanning the titles of the paintings Brunelleschi sent to the Salons up to the year 1910, one has the impression that he followed several poetic genres at the same time: besides portraits, we find references to undoubtedly Tuscan landscapes and paintings full of Symbolist feeling. A small round painting, datable before the end of 1905, belongs to this period: the brilliant colours are laid on flat and the subject is a half-length figure of a woman, classically attired, beside a parrot. The work bears the entwined monogram UB (which he used up to 1906), and with its graphic brevity and clear-cut outline shows familiarity with the methods of Emile Bernard and Maurice Denis, as well as an acquaintance with German Symbolist painting. Somewhat similar is the Self Portrait with a Parrot, painted in 1907 and

Toilette d'après-midi

Fashion sketch for the "Journal des Dames et des Modes", *engraving coloured "au pochoir", 1914.*

published the following year in a special issue of the Florentine paper, Giornalino della Domenica.

In 1907 (the year in which Picasso and Braque proclaimed the principles of their new concept of space and form) Brunelleschi, encouraged by his Paris success and returning for a brief period to his own country, began working for a children's paper founded by Vamba and illustrating children's books, but much of this work was of little worth compared to what he had been doing in Paris.

Shrill colouring and an alarming "heroic" subject, typical of the Symbolism of Hans von Marées and Max Klinger, are the main characteristics of the large painting called Automne, which Brunelleschi, once more in Paris, sent to the Salon des Indépendants in 1910. A few months earlier, at the Salon d'Automne, the young painter had exhibited some pictures inspired by the eighteenth-century Venice of Paul Verlaine's Fêtes Galantes. These canvases were full of jealous Harlequins, faithless Columbines and betrayed Pierrots immersed in an atmosphere of comic languor or sorrow. By choosing these subjects Brunelleschi started on a new road very different from that of the various avant-garde tendencies in painting, which on the one hand were attempting to extol modern technology and on the other were actively defining new spatial dimensions. But this predilection for fairy-tale and dream was the result of particular historical and spiritual needs. Europe at this time was suffering from broad rifts and profound social and political ferment. The middle classes, basking in the last warmth of the Belle Époque, were prey to a feeling of insecurity and they sought refuge in the lukewarm but witty evocation of an unreal, fabulous world. This sentimental trend toward escapism and spiritual withdrawal was congenial to Brunelleschi's nature, and he became one of its most gifted and successful interpreters.

Nor were eighteenth-century subjects, Venetianism,

BRUNELLESCHI

Robe à volant de satin brodé.

Fashion sketch for the "Journal des Dames et des Modes". engraving coloured "au pochoir", 1914.

and a taste for the costumes of the Commedia dell'Arte the rediscovery of Brunelleschi. They already existed, having been kept alive throughout the ninenteenth century by the Italian theatre, which had never ceased to represent the characters so dear to Watteau and Longhi. There had been many signs of interest in such subjects in the second half of the nineteenth century.

In 1859 the Goncourt brothers had published the catalogue of Watteau's works, almost forgotten during the Neoclassical and Romantic periods. In the same year an excellent work on the Commedia dell'Arte, Masques et Bouffons had appeared; it was written by Maurice Sand, George Sand's son, with a preface by his celebrated mother. The book contained a magnificent series of colour engravings of the historical development of the Commedia dell'Arte costumes. In 1860 the characters reappeared in painting: in Honoré Daumier's Crispino et Scapino (about ten years later, in Pierrot Playing the Guitar, he was to anticipate the sorrowful poetry of Georges Rouault).

In the years that followed, Venice with its lagoons, its serenades on the Grand Canal, its rose-hued palaces reflected in the green waters, its gondolas, love, costumes and mysterious starry nights was to provide painters and illustrators with an endless repertory of subjects. It is enough to mention Louis Morin[9], painter, illustrator and also writer, who in 1885 published Le cabaret du Puits sans Vin, representing a carnival with Venetian costumes and who, before illustrating his Amours de Gilles, went to Venice and spent long hours before the paintings in the Museo Corer. Another was Jules Chéret[10], with his evocations of a polite and melancholy Venice: he was the creator of the wall poster and had a liking for the quick sketch, typical of eighteenth-century painting. Sòme of his paintings, such as Domino jaune, and pastels, such as Pierrot mandoliniste, as well as numerous drawings of

Un po' di Colore (A bit of colour): costume for William Acton, tempera and madder on paper, 1915, Florence, Acton collection.

Un po' di Colore: sketch for scenery of the first scene, tempera on paper, 1915, Florence, Acton collection.

costumes inspired Brunelleschi, not with their style – the Frenchman's style was sprightly and vibrant while that of the Italian was steady and clear-cut – but with their iconography.

There is other evidence as well for the popularity of eighteenth-century Venetian subjects: in 1906 Alexander Benois, painter and designer for the Diaghilev group, presented three works of Venetian inspiration at the Russian Exhibition. Nor is this surprising if one thinks of the taste for fable and legend to be found in the work of Roerich[12], Bilibin[13], and Benois himself. In 1910 Leonetto Cappiello exhibited a painting at the Salon representing "a Paris cemetery covered with snow and three acrobats, Pierrot, Harlequin and Columbine, laying a wreath of flowers on the tomb of their dancing master"[14]. But the liking for fairy-tale and legendary subjects was not limited to those of Venice and the eighteenth-century: there was also the East - no longer Japan, as at the time of Art Nouveau, but India and Persia[15] – which kindled the imagination of artists.

Another important innovation around 1910 was the work in fashion of the couturier Poiret (the introduction of long dresses, either in the tunic style or high-waisted, uncorseted, and worn with turbans). At the same time came a revolution in colour schemes; this was begun by Bakst with the multicoloured glamour of his ballet Cleopatra, and then exploded in the incredible richness of colour of the scenery and costumes for Shéhérazade[16].

Thus themes of gallantry, sentiment, and eighteenth-century grace merged in these years with a bold and fanciful East and did not fail to produce some bizarre results even in everyday life (Lucie Delarue-Mardrus, wife of the translator of the Thousand and One Nights *and herself a writer, considered it perfectly appropriate to appear at the ball for Orphelinat des Arts in 1912 dressed as an Arab sheik and riding a horse[17]; she repeated the exploit in 1914 at a party in Venetian fancy dress given in Brunelleschi's house).*

In 1912 Barbier, Brunelleschi, and Lepape did the colour plates representing respectively La Comédie française, La Comédie italienne, *and* La Comédie persane *for the Christmas issue of the magazine* Fémina. *In these years Brunelleschi's activities became more intense and various. He devoted himself successfully to book illustration, advertising posters, fashion design and painting. For Fémina he did a number of front covers as well as advertising drawings in black and white (for Lubin perfumes and Perséphone corsets), showing the ever-present influence of the incisive lettering style of Beardsley, who was a point of reference for the leading illustrators of the time, from Lepape to Barbier, Maximilian Fischer, and Iribe. Yet it was Iribe who in the cover he did in 1910 for* Shéhérazade, *the magazine founded by Jean Cocteau, showed that, under the influence of the great English draughtsman, he had altered his style and achieved a refinement which, as it has already been rightly observed[18], influenced Brunelleschi's work in the plates that he was to do from 1912 on for the* Journal des Dames et des Modes[19].

In 1912, the year in which he illustrated Charles Perrault's Contes du Temps Jadis, *luxuriously published by Piazza (a work which shows his debt to a variety of sources, from the pre-Raphaelites through Rackham and Dulac, of whom the involved and repetitive style is a constant reminder),*

Ex Libris of William Acton, *tempera and madder on paper, 1915, Florence, Acton collection.*

Brunelleschi was summoned by Madame Rasimi, a leading actress-manager of the time, to create the costumes for a revue to be staged at the Bouffes Parisiens theatre. The effects of the innovations made by Diaghilev's team of designers – particularly Léon Bakst – were still very much alive.

With the brilliant and lively colours of his creations, the Petersburg artist had completely revolutionized both scenery and costumes, up till then bound by strict ideas of line and colour deriving from traditional nineteenth-century oleographic canons (similarly in Italy, such artists as Carlo Songa, Antonio Rovescalli, Mario Sala, and Alessandro Parravicini[20], with meticulous attention to historical detail and slavish following of traditional realism, had created vast stage sets filled with minutiae but lacking focal interest). In his fantastic and ever-changing costumes Bakst drew inspiration from Persian miniatures and Indian and Siamese painting, as well as from the icons and folk art of his own country.

Bakst had an almost instantaneous effect on Barbier, whose decisive and controlled draughtsmanship can be seen in the illustrations for Makeda, Reine de Saba, published by Goupil in 1914, on Georges Lepape (author in 1911 of a famous album for Poiret), supple, free and ironical in style; and finally on Brunelleschi himself, though he was always inclined to soften outspoken colour by his delicacy of line and image. In 1914, before leaving for the front, Brunelleschi created designs for Madame Rasimi's revue Y'a d'Jolies Femmes. The set for the first act, entitled La légende de Pierre de Lune or La Comédie italienne, was his. The subject was most congenial to the sensibility and taste of the Italian artist, who the previous year had had much success with his illustrations for Alfred de Musset's La nuit Vénitienne and Les Caprices de Marianne.

Madame Rasimi's revue contained no less than seventeen scenes, but the one by Brunelleschi,

Un po' di Colore: costume for Cora Antinori, tempera on paper, 1915, Florence, Chigiotti collection.

created for Venetian characters, was the most
successful. The Petit Parisien *critic wrote: "The
Italian Comedy scenery, designed from sketches by
the painter Brunelleschi, is certainly the most
magnificent and daring thing to be produced by the
theatre since the celebrated sketches by Bakst".*
In the same year the directors of the Journal des
Dames et des Modes *asked Brunelleschi to design a
large album illustrating the costumes and characters
of the Commedia dell'Arte with colour plates
au pochoir (a technique using cardboard stencils,
that was to be the subject of an entire treatise by
Jean Saudé in 1925). The volume was called*
Les Masques et les Personnages de la Comédie
italienne *and enjoyed enormous success.*
*Looking through the pages, one is reminded of Paul
Verlaine's lines:*
"Scaramouche et Pulcinelle
Qu'un mauvais dessein rassemble
Gesticulent, noirs sous la lune.
Cependant que le vieux docteur
Bolonais cueille avec lenteur
Des simples, parmi l'herbe brune..."
*There seems to be no end to the variety of
Brunelleschi's style here: in the portrayal of Pierrot
it flows with an essential calm, only to open out in
rhythmic loops and curls, as in the figure of
Pantalone; sometimes it becomes complicated and
takes on a calligraphic refinement, as in Florindo,
giving the figures a fantastic and trembling
sensitivity which is accentuated by the unreal quality
of the flat colours. We seem to be in the presence of
a less evil Beardsley who impels our imagination
towards a lost paradise of memories and fantasy.
Barbier too showed an interest in such subjects:
his illustrations for* Personnages de Comédie *(1922)
had less enchantment of colour and a generally
quieter style, though plates like that of Turandot*[23]
*show considerable imagination; later on Barbier was
to return to Venetian subjects with his pleasant but*

Au Bon Marché, *sketch for an advertising poster, tempera on
paper, 1925/1930, Rome, private collection.*

Fashion sketch, *pencil and tempera on paper, ca. 1930,
Rome, private collection.*

less sensitive illustrations for Verlaine's Les Fêtes Galantes.

In 1914 Brunelleschi appeared at the Venice Biennale with tempera illustrations on eighteenth-century subjects taken from the Contes and La Nuit Vénitienne and the completed series of originals for the costumes published by the Journal des Dames et des Modes. He also exhibited a large realistic picture that failed to win the approval of Ugo Ojetti, who wrote in his review of the Biennale[24]: "Notable among the other Tuscans [is]... the refined and delightful Brunelleschi, who reveals his imaginative and literary taste in watercolours illustrating comedies by De Musset and fairy stories by Perrault rather than in the big oil painting of a mulatto woman depicted against a deep blue background beside a yellow monkey dressed in green; the painstakingly detailed and realistic style of this work ill matches the violent and fanciful colours".
Meanwhile Brunelleschi's fame as a costume designer had reached Florence, where his name was constantly heard in aristocratic and fashionable circles. He was asked to design the scenery and costumes for a Red Cross charity entertainment to be staged at the Pergola Theatre on 17 March 1915. The entertainment consisted of two plays, Le Falene (The Moths) and Un po' di colore (A Bit of Colour), both by Vincenzo Sorelli; the actors included some of Florence's most aristocratic names: Sir Harold Acton, a boy at the time, was present and retained vivid memories of the occasion[25]: "Already in March (1915) the Florentines had organized a revue for the Red Cross at The Pergola Theatre, in which sympathy for the Allies was pronounced. My mother and my brother both took part in it, and it was far more than the title announced, A bit of colour, for Umberto Brunelleschi had designed·the costumes and settings as he had been doing successfully for the Folies-Bergère in Paris".
In the first scene Brunelleschi had conceived a

*highly colourful background showing the
amphitheatre of Fiesole overhung with enormous
blue cypress trees. The blazing colours left no doubt
as to the influence of the great Bakst, who was to be
in Florence soon after with his company[26]. The most
successful costumes were those designed for the
Marchesa Cappelli, who played Pisanella and
D'Annunzio's Muse, and still more those of the lovely
Cora Antinori[27], who was completely at her ease in
the parts of the Maeterlinck's Muse and the Queen
of Fashion.*

*Though a volunteer in the Italian Third Army,
Brunelleschi did not miss any opportunity for work,
even in wartime: he sent in drawings for* La Tradotta,
*worked for more illustrated magazines and painted
(as can be seen from the portrait of Emmanuel
Philibert of Savoy done at the front). While he was
in service he was asked to design the scenery and
costumes for* Il Carillon magico, *a ballet with music
by Riccardo Pick-Mangiagalli composed for la Scala
in Milan.*

*The subject of the ballet would seem to have been
made for Brunelleschi: Venetian characters. It was
performed in 1918 and met with great success, less
for the musical ability of the composer than for
the brilliant dancing of Lucia Cignaroli and the
contribution of Brunelleschi. The scenery (black-and-
white chequer-board decoration with a central
perspective, gilded trees and typical Art Deco motifs)
and the costumes roused the admiration of the
public. The result was that Mangiagalli asked
Brunelleschi to work with him on the ballet
Sumitra[28], taken from an Indian legend, and which
was produced the following year.*

*After the war, Brunelleschi returned to Paris and
continued working for the féerie theatres and
music halls, where he now had the company and
also the rivalry of the whimsical and elegant
Russian, Romain Tirtoff, known as Erté, who had
made his mark in 1917 with his costumes created for*

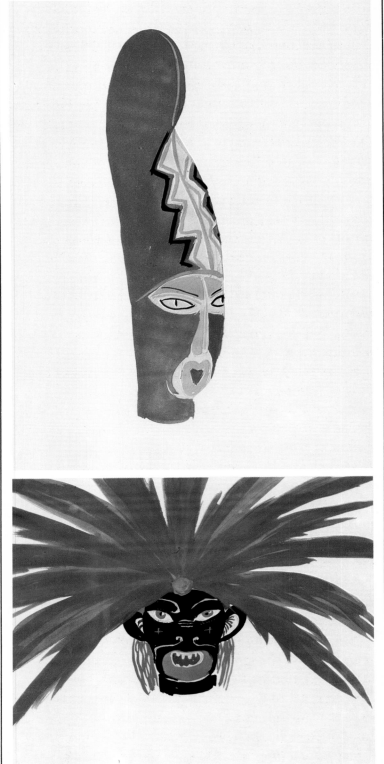

Mistinguett in L'Orient merveilleux. *Around 1920 Brunelleschi's fame was enormous: numerous artists, including some Italians (for example, Ettore Tito and Francesco Nonni) and the promising young Maria de' Matteis[29] who later became a highly gifted costume designer, found inspiration in his Venetian subjects. In spite of his theatrical work, Brunelleschi continued to paint: between 1916 and 1920 he produced a number of works including fantasies on eighteenth-century subjects such as* Carnevale *and a few excellent portraits, though nothing, of course, that showed any avant-garde influence. (These were the years in which De Chirico painted* Hector and Andromache, *Morandi did the* Still Life *in the Mattioli collection, and Carrà conceived his* Drunken Gentleman, *moving on after his metaphysical phase to a renewed classicism and traditionalism which appeared magnificently in his famous* Pine Tree by the Sea, *painted in 1921). His proximity to the Symbolist ideal can still be seen in the radiant portrait of his wife, Camille, depicting her almost in profile while a horse's head appears unbelievably from the surrounding foliage. The portrait of his sister and that of the Venetian Countess Vera Arrivabene (exhibited at the 1920 Venice Biennale) show a variety of influences. The former betrays an interest in Matisse's arabesques and the figurative style of Picasso, while the latter shows signs of Japanese feeling (the beautifully embroidered shawl) and a bold composition reminiscent of Mario Cavaglieri[30]. Brunelleschi's work as a costume designer was now reaching its most important period: the years between 1925 and 1935 were those of his greatest success, even though he was competing with such highly talented artists as Erté, Barbier, Lepape, Zinoviev, Betout and Zamora. Early in the twenties the* Paris Music-hall *critic had written of the revue* En Pleine Folie, *performed at the Folies-Bergère: "Never have the Folies-Bergère treated us to such*

splendour. For all the decoration and costumes, this time we must thank M. Lemarchand for having secured the services of such artists as Messieurs Erté, Montedoro, Dolly, Tree, Aumond, Zinoviev and above all the exquisite Monsieur Brunelleschi".

In 1924 Brunelleschi's fame reached the ears of Giacomo Puccini, who wrote to the artist:
"Dear Brunelleschi, Turandot is nearly finished. I am thinking of you for the costume sketches. Can you, will you, do them for me? I do hope so. I am most anxious to have your art coupled with mine. For the scenery I have thought of Galileo Chini, who I think, will do something good and original. The opera is powerful and in some parts bizarre. It must be a remote and very ancient China. I hope that your art and Chini's will combine well. When will you be coming to Italy? It is important for us three to meet. The publisher Ricordi has approved my choice of collaborators. I look forward to having a line from you in reply, and consent..."

Brunelleschi prepared highly fanciful costumes for the opera, which was performed in 1926 at La Scala; they were later published in a book by Ricordi. Unfortunately, on the pretext of a delay in the delivery of the last sketches, the opera was performed with costumes by Caramba[33], an old-fashioned artist and far less gifted than Brunelleschi, who was, however, the official designer for the Milan opera house. Meanwhile around 1925, Art Deco began to assert itself without opposition. With its geometrical linearity and conciseness it had a profound influence on all branches of the applied arts. This was also the period in which Josephine Baker arrived in Paris, along with Afro-American music. Even the exotic was changing key. In 1928 the dancer Léonide Massine, who knew Brunelleschi well, asked him[34] to create four new ballets for the opening of the Roxy Theater in New York. Brunelleschi was also responsible for the stage direction of the ballets, which were entitled:

La Gondole Rouge, Les Masques en Chine, Le Prince Charmant et Fiammetta, *and* Mademoiselle Angot. *Thus in spite of the changes in taste brought by the* revue nègre, *China and Venice, those abodes of Brunelleschian mythology, continued to win success. In the late twenties Brunelleschi's style began showing signs of alteration. It can be seen in his covers for fashion magazines, in his advertisements for* Au Bon Marché / Maison A. Boucicaut, *and particularly in certain tempera drawings depicting fashionable Parisian life. His former linearity tends to diminish or to cease altogether; his colours become more substantial and less fanciful, and his draughtsmanship aims at more realistic effects through nuance and shading; gradually his designs become geometrically interlocking bands of colour. In this period Brunelleschi had much in common with Erté and Benito, from whom the Italian Sto[35] took his characteristic elongated, outlined style. Even after 1930 Brunelleschi's theatrical activities continued with great success. Many of the costumes for Josephine Baker's revues were created by him. These shows often contained scenes betraying the presence of his specialized hand, as in "Un soir au bal à Florence" which was part of* L'Usine à Folies, *given at the Folies-Bergère in 1931. Offenbach's operetta* Créole, *performed in 1934 at the Théâtre Marigny with Josephine Baker, was another happy example. Yet though he continued to show unusual talent in his theatrical work, a decline had begun in the quality of his illustrations. Those for* Radjad de Mazulipatam, *done in 1926, were already very inferior to those of* Phili au Par de là le Bien et le Mal, *done five years earlier[5]. As the years went by his style grew heavier and fluctuated between sentimentality and oleographic meticulousness. Some of his minor works were better: slightly risqué postcards of sparsely dressed women show a pleasing sense of humour extremely rare in Brunelleschi. His decline as a painter was to become obvious only*

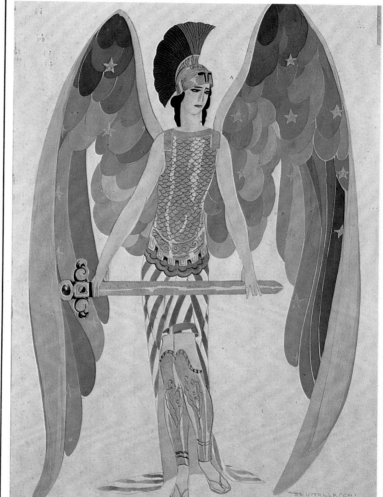

21

in the forties. A sad example of this was the one-man show, the last in his lifetime, held in Brussels in 1947. His best paintings done between 1930 and 1940, like Doctor Ballanzone *(1933), a still-life with masks and musical instruments seen against a landscape, are inspired by a moderate realism with occasional flights of fancy that was fairly common in the thirties and was linked to a bourgeois poetic theory that had various champions in Tuscany – Guido Peyron, Gordigiani, Gianni Vagnetti, and Baccio Maria Bacci. The self-portrait painted in 1938,* La Commedia è finita *(The Play is over), is the last painting to show his quality as an artist: Brunelleschi depicts himself dressed as Pulcinella in the act of taking off his mask, beside a fantastic stage curtain that gives a glimpse of Tuscan hills in the background. The picture is of unquestionably good workmanship and is remarkable for the warmth of the paint, the control, and the balanced composition.*

The success of his theatrical production showed no sign of fading, even when the revue *became Americanized and the Blue Bells arrived in Paris. Brunelleschi continued to work with those theatres that had been receiving and acclaiming his work for twenty years. Between 1934 and 1940 he was kept busy by the Folies-Bergère* (Folies en Folies; Femmes en Folie; En Super-folies), *the Châtelet* (Au soleil du Mexique), *and the Mogador* (Balalaika). *But his swan song, after the success of* The Pearl Fishermen *given at La Scala in 1938, was in his native Florence: the scenery and costumes for Puccini's* Turandot, *presented during the Maggio Musicale in 1940. Italian theatre design had made considerable progress, thanks largely to the astute artistic policy of the Florentine theatre, which, with the object of reviving and stimulating drama, had enlisted the services of the leading painters of the time as set and costume designers: De Chirico, Casorati, Carena and Sironi. In addition to these,*

several excellent professionals such as Gino Sensani and the young Maria de' Matteis were also working in the field. Thus with Turandot Brunelleschi was, in a way, comparing his work as veteran artist with that of the new painter-scenographers. It was a comparison in which he came out well. The first scene, showing the barriers in Peking, was forceful not only for its striking colour but also for its vigour and terseness of line. The scenery of the second act betrayed something of Brunelleschi's penchant for fairy-tale, even if in a "modernized" key (the outlines of the pink and blue trees were unforgettable). But the most extraordinary thing was the costumes: these were all of astounding beauty, in georgeous colours, fantastic without being abstruse.

Even those of the minor characters were designed with the greatest care down to the last detail. The splendid figures of the warriors and those of the common people wearing masks of fantastic animals showed that Brunelleschi had drawn on ancient Asiatic and Chinese art. These were the words of the critic for the Florentine paper La Nazione: "Umberto Brunelleschi has conjured up a dazzling Turandot: his fantastical ingenuity, marked by an elegant richness of form and colour, has been allowed to fulfill itself in the portrayal of the Chinese surroundings in which the unusual plot unfolds to the music of Giacomo Puccini. This is a dream China, a phantasmagoric fairy-tale vision, with elements of the Commedia dell'Arte in the second act and a broad, mysterious nocturnal landscape in the third. The costumes are infinitely charming and designed with meticulous care, as is Brunelleschi's habit: the two belonging to Princess Turandot, the witty one of the judge, those of the masked characters, and the lovely dancers' array, will, I believe, be greatly admired; the warrior figures seem to be taken from ancient Oriental prints". The Second World War swept away the artist's fairy-tale world. Ignored and forgotten, Brunelleschi

now pitifully tired went on illustrating a few books and painting a few pictures before he died on 16 February, 1949. In 1928 a Paris critic had written what was perhaps his finest elegy: "His art has nothing realistic about it. He would not know how to evoke modern life with its huge factories and streets full of people. But the world of fiction, which is so much more beautiful than the world of men, that he makes real".

Cristina Nuzzi

Notes

1. *Cf. G. Ercoli,* Brunelleschi, *Florence, 1978.*

2. *Giuseppe Ciaranfi (Pistoia 1838 - Florence 1902) and Raffaello Sorbi (Florence 1844 - 1931), the former a pupil of Enrico Pollastrini and the latter of Antonio Ciseri, painted realistic works on subjects drawn from ancient, medieval, and eighteenth-century history.*

3. *In 1879 Diego Martelli gave a lecture at the Philological Club in Leghorn on the Impressionists; it was published the following year in Pisa: see also* Scritti d'arte, *selected and edited by A. Boschetto, Florence, 1952.*

4. *Alfredo Muller attended the Paris studio of Carolus-Duran, an academic painter, but was also in touch with Pissarro and Cézanne and became the spokesman for neo-Impressionist theories in Italy.*

5. *Gino Melis joined Brunelleschi, Soffici, and Costetti later; cf. A. Soffici,* Salto Vitale, *Florence, 1954, p. 170; Melis was a lively reporter on Paris.*

6. *Paul Iribe (1883-1935): in these illustrations he shows a tangled style of drawing, very different from the clear-cut manner of his later, famous album done for Paul Poiret,* Les robes de Paul Poiret racontés par Paul Iribe, *Paris, 1908.*

7. *The review of the exhibition at the Salon de la Société Nationale des Beaux-Arts appeared on 14 April 1906, in* L'Intransigeant.

8. *James Whistler (1834-1903) was often in Paris after 1855. In 1858, through Henri Fantin-Latour, he met Courbet and other French artists, with whom, in 1863, he exhibited* The White Girl *at the Salon des Refusés. Whistler had an enormous influence on painters such as Le Sidaner and Aman-Jean.*

9. *Louis Morin (1855-1936): his father, for twenty-five years tutor in the service of the Duke of Terranova in Naples, had taught him to love the Italian landscape.*

10. *Jules Chéret (1836-1933), described by Degas as "the Watteau of the streets", between 1890 and 1900 was*

doing drawings, pastels, and oil paintings of Venetian characters and eighteenth-century subjects.
cf. C. Mauclair, Jules Chéret, Paris, 1930.

11. The paintings on eighteenth-century subjects were: Le Pavillon Chinois or Le Jaloux (No. 70); La Comédie Italienne, Polichinelle indiscret (No. 71); La Comédie Italienne, Le billet doux (No. 72).

12. Nicolas Roerich (1874-1942), painter and scenographer for the Diaghilev company, is to be remembered for his determined attachment to fairy-tale motifs, which he interpreted in a crude manner derived from Russian folk art.

13. Ivan Bilibin (1876-1942), another painter employed by Diaghilev, was an imaginative draughtsman of great talent and was influenced by Art Nouveau; in 1905 he illustrated one of Pushkin's stories, "The Tale of Czar Saltan", combining a linearity of Japanese origin with subjects taken from Russian folklore.

14. From the Gazzetta di Torino, 13 December 1910.

15. The taste for the Persian and Indian East was encouraged, before Bakst and Poiret, by Dr. Mardrus' French translation of the Thousand and One Nights; this was followed by an exhibition of watercolours on the same subject by the painter Edmund Dulac (1882-1953), held in London in 1907.

16. The ballet, interpreted by Vaslav Nijisnky and Ida Rubinstein, was performed at the Châtelet theatre on 4 June 1910.

17. Reported in Fémina, 1 July 1912; the cover shows a photograph of Lucie Delarue-Mardrus on horseback dressed as an Arab chieftain.

18. G. Veronesi, Stile 1925, Florence, 1966, p. 48.

19. This highly sophisticated fashion paper was started in Paris under the auspices of Gabriele D'Annunzio by Tom Antongini, the Italian poet's friend and secretary who was also a writer and viveur.

20. Antonio Rovescalli (1864-1936), Carlo Songa (1856-1911), Mario Sala (1873-1920) and Alessandro Parravicini (1868-1925) were all scenographers who worked for La Scala.

21. As far back as the eighteenth century, colouring au patron and au pochoir meant applying colour with the help of stencils: in the first case it was done with a brush and in the second it was sprayed by blowing through a pipe. In the first decades of this century the term "pochoir" was used to describe hand-coloured printing in general, without distinguishing between the two techniques ("patron" was used to describe large surfaces and "pochoir" for more delicate colouring).

22. Paul Verlaine, Fêtes Galantes, Paris, 1869.

23. G. Barbier, Personnages de Comédie, Paris, 1922.

24. U. Ojetti, L'Undicesima Esposizione Internazionale d'Arte in Venezia, Venice, 1914.

25. H. Acton, Memoirs of an Aesthete, London, 1948.

26. The Diaghilev company, with its most famous scenographer Léon Bakst, was en tournée in Florence in 1917.

27. Cora Antinori, leading light of society life at the time; on 25 May 1915 Brunelleschi painted a fine portrait of her in profile: the elegant style, the sweeping representation of light and shade, and the delicate "découpé" outline showed clear signs of French influence.

28. According to a letter from C. Clausetti to Brunelleschi dated 19 May 1919 (Brunelleschi archive), the original title of the ballet was Gandshari and it went on the stage in 1919.

29. Maria de' Matteis, who later made an exceptional career as costume designer, exhibited some colour drawings at the 1920 Venice Biennale, the tones of which resembled Brunelleschi's brilliant-hued fantasies: cf. F. Sapori, L'Arte mondiale alla XII esposizione di Venezia - 1920, Bergamo, pp. 232-233.

30. Mario Cavaglieri (1887-1969): after a stay in France in 1911 he altered his style, under the influence of the "coquetterie" of Chahine and Helleu - for example L'Aigrette, 1912 - the teachings of the Impressionists and the Intimist interiors of Bonnard and Vuillard.

31. In Paris Music-Hall, 1 April 1923.

32. Letter from Giacomo Puccini to Umberto Brunelleschi dated 26 February 1924 (Brunelleschi archive).

33. Cf. the article on "Caramba and Turandot" in La Stampa

(Turin) 15 November 1937.

34. *Letter from Léonide Massine to Umberto Brunelleschi, dated 2 December 1928 (Brunelleschi archive).*

35. *Sto, alias Sergio Tofano (1886-1973), actor and writer whose fame as an illustrator is due to his celebrated character Bonaventura; he was influenced by the style of French illustrators, particularly Lepape and Benito, as may be seen in the terse effectiveness of his delicate, elongated lines, found in the illustrations for some covers of* Numero, *1915 (No. 104) and 1916 (Nos. 121 and 144).*

36. *In 1938 the painting was shown at the Venice Biennale; cf.* Catalogo della XXI Biennale di Venezia, *Venice, 1938, p. 123, No. 15.*

List of Plates

Le Docteur Ballanzone

Florindo

Brighella

Coralline

Pantalon

Tartaglia

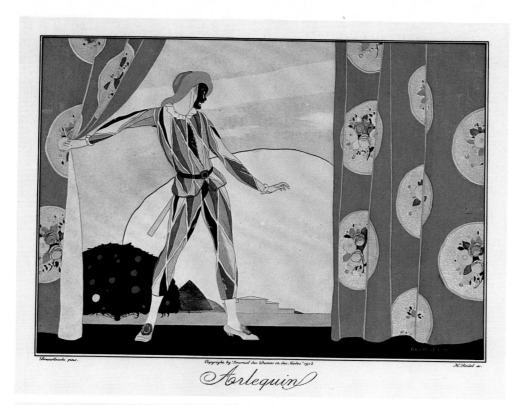

Arlequin

Rosdura

Mezzetin et Colombine

Scaramouche

Brunelleschi pinx.   Copyright by "Journal des Dames et des Modes" 1914   *H. Reidel sc.*

Giacometta

Brunelleschi pinx.   Copyright by "Journal des Dames et des Modes" 1914   *H. Reidel sc.*

Trivellino

37

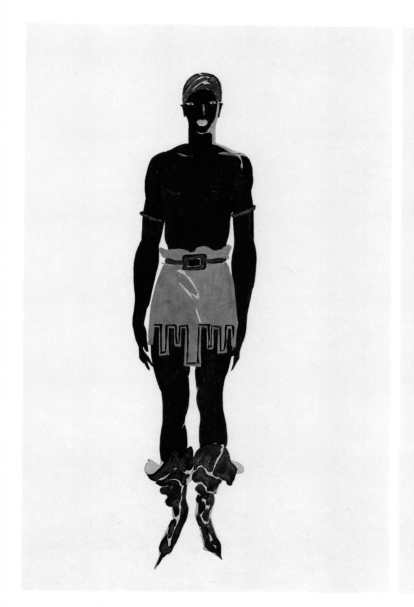

Poste d'observation

BRUNELLESCHI

PRIMAVERA

Le matin s'est envolé   Et de là ne rêve qu'une chose
de sa belle cage rouge.   se blottir entre les bouts
sur une branche il s'est posé de tes seins teintes de rose

Le Comparse

BRUNELLESCHI